The material was previously published in the book *Pet Projects: The Animal Knits Bible* (ISBN 978-1-60085-127-8) first published in 2007 by Quadrille Publishing Limited Alhambra House, 27-31 Charing Cross Road, London, WC2H 0LS

First published in this format 2013

The Taunton Press
Inspiration for hands-on living®

The Taunton Press, Inc., 63 South Main Street, PO Box 5506, Newtown, CT 06470-5506
e-mail: tp@taunton.com

Cover Design: Kimberly Adis
Interior Design: © 2007 Quadrille Publishing Limited
Photographer: Diana Miller

Threads® is a trademark of The Taunton Press, Inc., registered in the U.S. Patent and Trademark Office.

Library of Congress Cataloging-in-Publication Data

Muir, Sally.
 Pet projects to knit : perfect projects for pampered pets / Sally Muir and Joanna Osborne.
   pages cm
  ISBN 978-1-62710-099-1 (pbk.)
1. Knitting--Patterns. 2. Pet supplies. I. Osborne, Joanna. II. Title.
 TT825.M7853 2013
 746.43'2--dc23

Printed in the United States of America
10 9 8 7 6 5 4 3 2 1

Table of Cor

HAMSTER HOUSE

LEVEL
Easy

SIZE
The finished hamster house measures approximately 11³/4in/29.5cm in circumference by 4¹/2in/11.5cm tall, not including tassel at top.

MATERIALS
Light/DK Weight Yarn (CYCA 3), approx. 130 yds in color of your choice (shown in *Rowan Scottish Tweed Aran*) in main color **MC** for house
Small amount of a fine weight yarn in a contrasting color **A**, for tassel
Pair of size 5 (3.75mm) knitting needles
Crochet hook, for attaching tassel

GAUGE
19 sts and 27 rows to 4in/10cm measured over St st using size 5 (3.75mm) needles.
Note: The house is knitted tighter than suggested on the yarn label so that it is firm enough to stand up.

ABBREVIATIONS
See page 30.

TO MAKE HOUSE
With size 5 (3.75mm) needles and MC, cast on 56 sts.
Work 6 rows in garter stitch (knit every row).
Mark each end of last row with a colored thread.
Cont in garter st, bind off 3 sts at beg of each of next 2 rows, then 2 sts at beg of 2 foll rows. (46 sts.)
Work even in garter st for 6 rows.
Cont in garter st, cast on 2 sts at beg of each of next 2 rows, then 3 sts at beg of 2 foll rows. (56 sts.)
Mark each end of last row with a colored thread.
Work even in garter st for 8 rows.

Shape top
Change to St st and shape top of house as follows:
Next row (RS) [K2tog, k5] 8 times. (48 sts.)
Purl 1 row.
Next row [K2tog, k4] 8 times. (40 sts.)
Purl 1 row.
Next row [K2tog, k3] 8 times. (32 sts.)
Purl 1 row.
Next row [K2tog, k2] 8 times. (24 sts.)
Purl 1 row.
Next row [K2tog, k1] 8 times. (16 sts.)
Purl 1 row.
Next row [K2tog] 8 times. (8 sts.)
Purl 1 row.
Next row [K2tog] 4 times. (4 sts.)
Purl 1 row.
Next row [K2tog] twice. (2 sts.)
Next row P2tog, then break off MC, thread tail end through rem st, and pull tight to fasten off.

TO FINISH
Do not press.
Join house at center front to form it into a circle as follows:
With right sides together, sew together side edges of knitting between cast-on edge and first set of markers; then sew together side edges of knitting between second set of markers and top point of house. Turn right side out.

Tassel
Cut five strands of A, each 4in/10cm long. Holding strands together, fold them in half and use a crochet hook to pull loop at folded end of strands through top of house. Still using hook, pull ends of strands through loop, then pull ends tight to secure tassel in place.
Trim ends of tassel to desired length.

MOUSE MAT FOR CAT

LEVEL
Easy

SIZE
The finished mouse mat measures approximately 15³/₄in/40cm wide across the body and 29¹/₂in/75cm long from nose to tail.

Note: If your cat is enormous, you can make the mat bigger by adding more stitches and rows in the center.

MATERIALS
Super Bulky Weight Yarn (CYCA 6), approx. 218 yds in man color **MC** for mat and back of ears. (Shown in *Rowan Scottish Tweed Chunky*)
Small amount of same yarn in contrasting color **A**, for inside of ears, nose, and whiskers
Small amount of double-knitting-weight yarn that matches **MC**, for sewing ear fronts to ear backs
Pair of size 11 (8mm) knitting needles
2 black buttons, for eyes
Crochet hook, for attaching whiskers

GAUGE
11 sts and 19 rows to 4in/10cm measured over garter st using size 11 (8mm) needles.

ABBREVIATIONS
See page 30.

TO MAKE MOUSE MAT
The whole body and tail of mouse mat is knitted in garter st, starting at tail end.

Shape tail
With size 11 (8mm) needles and MC, cast on 2 sts.
Work 12 rows in garter st (knit every row).
Cont in garter st throughout, inc 1 st at each end of next row. *(4 sts.)*
Work even for 11 rows.
Inc 1 st at each end of next row. *(6 sts.)*
Work even for 11 rows.

Begin body
Cast on 12 sts at end of next 2 rows. *(30 sts.)*
Work even for 1 row.

Inc 1 st at each end of next 9 rows. *(48 sts.)*
Work even for 2 rows.

Shape back legs
**Cast on 10 sts at end of next 2 rows. *(68 sts.)*
Inc 1 st at each end of next 3 rows. *(74 sts.)*
Work even for 4 rows.
Dec 1 st at each end of next 3 rows. *(68 sts.)*
Bind off 11 sts at beg of next 2 rows. *(46 sts.)***
Work even for 36 rows.

Shape front legs
Rep from ** to ** once more.

Work even for 1 row. *(44 sts.)*

Shape neck and head
Bind off 5 sts at beg of next 2 rows. *(34 sts.)*
Bind off 4 sts at beg of next 2 rows. *(26 sts.)*
Bind off 2 sts at beg of next 2 rows. *(22 sts.)*
Work even for 4 rows.
Dec 1 st at each end of next row and then at each end of 2 foll 4th rows. *(16 sts.)*
Dec 1 st at each end of 3 foll alt rows. *(10 sts.)*
Dec 1 st at each end of next 4 rows. *(2 sts.)*
Work even for 2 rows.
Next row K2tog, then break off yarn,

thread tail end through rem st, and pull to fasten off.

EAR BACKS (MAKE 2)

With size 11 (8mm) needles and MC, cast on 6 sts.

Beg with a k row, work 2 rows in St st, ending with a p row.

Cont in St st throughout, inc 1 st at each end of next row. (8 sts.)

Work even for 5 rows, ending with a p row.

Dec 1 st at each end of next row and then at each end of foll alt row, ending with a k row. (4 sts.)

Work even for 1 row.

Bind off.

Make a second ear back in same way.

EAR FRONTS (MAKE 2)

With size 11 (8mm) needles and A, cast on 5 sts.

Work 2 rows in garter st.

Cont in garter st throughout, inc 1 st at each end of next row. (7 sts.)

Work even for 5 rows.

Dec 1 st at each end of next row and then at each end of foll alt row. (3 sts.)

Work even for 1 row.

Bind off.

Make a second ear front in same way.

TO FINISH

Using double-knitting yarn, sew fronts of ears to backs. Sew ears to mouse's head, parallel to front legs and approximately 3in/7.5cm apart. Lightly press ear backs on wrong side, following instructions on yarn label and avoiding garter st.

Nose, whiskers, and eyes

Using a blunt-ended yarn needle and A, sew tip of head over and over to make nose. For whiskers, cut eight 4in/10cm lengths of A. Fold one length in half and use a crochet hook to pull looped end through edge of mat 1/4in/6mm from nose; pull ends of yarn through loop and tighten. Attach three more lengths of yarn A along edge of head and about 1/2in/12mm apart, working away from nose. Attach four whiskers on other side of nose in same way.

Sew on two buttons for eyes, about 2in/5cm apart and 1 1/2in/4cm from ears.

TASSELS **CAT** CUSHION

LEVEL
Easy

SIZE
The finished cushion measures approximately 18in/46cm square.

MATERIALS
Super Bulky Weight Yarn (CYC 6) approx. 327 yds in main color **MC**, for cushion (shown in *Rowan Scottish Tweed Chunky*)
Small amount of double-knitting-weight yarn in contrasting color **A**, for tassels
Pair of size 11 (8mm) knitting needles
Pillow form to fit

GAUGE
12 sts and 16 rows to 4in/10cm measured over St st using size 11 (8mm) needles.

ABBREVIATIONS
See page 30

TO MAKE CUSHION COVER
With size 11 (8mm) needles and MC, cast on 54 sts.
Beg with a k row, work in St st until cushion measures 36in/92cm from cast-on edge, ending with a p row.
Bind off.

TO FINISH
Press lightly on wrong side, following instructions on yarn label.
Sew cast-on edge of knitting to bound-off edge.

With cover right-side out, position seam just worked in center back of cushion; then sew one side seam using mattress stitch. Insert pillow form and sew other side seam in same way.

Tassels (make 4)
Cut a piece of cardboard 2in/5cm wide by 4in/10cm long.
Wind A around length of cardboard 25 times. Then thread a needle with a length of A and pass it under wrapped yarn at one end of cardboard. Tie yarn tightly, leaving two long tail ends. Cut through strands of yarn at other end of cardboard. Wind one long tail end of yarn tightly around tassel approximately 3/4in/2cm from uncut end and secure.
Use remaining length of yarn to sew tassel to one corner of cushion.
Make three more tassels in same way and sew one to each of the three remaining corners.

POMPOMS

LEVEL
Easy

SIZE
The finished pompoms measure approximately 3in/7.5cm in diameter.
Note: To alter the size of the pompoms, cut smaller or larger cardboard circles.

MATERIALS
Wool pompom
Assorted colors of double-knitting-weight yarn
Plastic pompom
One clear or colored plastic bag, to make "yarn"
Both pompoms
Cardboard—a cereal box is ideal

WOOL POMPOM

CARDBOARD POMPOM TEMPLATES (MAKE 2)
Using a compass or drawing around the base of a mug, draw a circle about 3in/7.5cm in diameter on the cardboard (the size of the circle will be the size of finished pompom). Draw a 1in/2.5cm circle in the center of the first circle. Cut out the larger circle, then cut out the small circle at the center.
Make a second cardboard circle exactly the same.

TO MAKE POMPOM
Hold the two cardboard circles together and wind the yarn around the ring as evenly as possible until the hole is almost closed up with yarn (it is quicker to wind several strands at once). Then thread yarn onto a needle and continue to wind until the hole is closed up.
Cut the yarn around the edge of the circles, sliding a point of the scissors along in between the two pieces of cardboard. Ease the cardboard templates slightly apart and wrap a long length of doubled yarn between the templates and around the center of the pompom. Tie the pompom together tightly at the center, leaving two long tail ends of yarn hanging.
Then pull, or cut, the cardboard away from the pompom.

Fluff up the pompom and trim into shape if necessary. For a hanging cord, twist the two long ends of yarn together and knot.

PLASTIC POMPOM

TO PREPARE PLASTIC "YARN"
Prepare the plastic "yarn" as for the Water Lily on page 18.

TO MAKE POMPOM
Make the cardboard templates and the pompom as for the wool pompom, but be careful not to tear the plastic "yarn" and use ordinary yarn to tie the pompom at the center.

BEANBAG **PET** BED

LEVEL
Knitted beanbag cover: Easy
Beanbag fabric cushion: Intermediate

SIZES
Choose your size as follows:
Small—for a cat
Medium—for a small/medium dog
Large—for a large dog

The finished beanbag measures approximately 22 (25: 28)in/ 55 (62.5: 70)cm in diameter across the circular base, and each of the four top segments (which form the top and sides of the bag) measures 17 (22: 27)in/43 (55.5: 68.5)cm from the cast-on edge to the tip at the center of the beanbag.

MATERIALS
Knitted beanbag cover
Aran/Medium Weight Yarn (CYCA 4), approx. 600 yds in a selection of 6 or more different colors (beanbag cushion shown is knit in 10–13 assorted colors of *Rowan Scottish Tweed Aran*, *Rowan Pure Wool DK*, and *Jaeger Matchmaker Merino DK*) See Special Yarn Note on following page
Pair of size 9 (5.5mm) knitting needles
4 large snaps
Beanbag cushion
Newspaper, or other large sheets of paper, for paper pattern
Approximately $2^{1}/4$ ($2^{1}/2$: $2^{3}/4$)yd/2 (2.2: 2.5)m of 45in/112cm wide calico or other cotton fabric remnant, and matching sewing thread
18in/45cm zipper
18oz/500g of polystyrene balls, for cushion filling

GAUGE
16 sts and 30 rows to 4in/10cm measured over garter stitch using size 9 (5.5mm) needles and Aran/Medium Weight Yarn.

ABBREVIATIONS
See page 30.

SPECIAL YARN NOTE

Use the Rowan *Scottish Tweed Aran* yarn **single** when knitting the beanbag, but use the Rowan *Pure Wool DK* or Jaeger *Matchmaker Merino DK* **double**. Use Jaeger *Fur* sparingly, introducing it across only one or two rows in the top segments of the beanbag.

The yarns specified are only suggestions, as this project provides an ideal opportunity for you to use up leftover yarns in a variety of textures—the more textured the beanbag, the more interesting it will be. Remember to use your leftover Aran-weight yarn single, your leftover double-knitting-weight yarn double, and very thick yarns (like the Jaeger *Fur*) only in a couple of rows.

Prepare the yarn as explained before beginning your knitting.

KNITTED BEANBAG COVER

TO PREPARE THE YARN

Cut the Aran-weight yarn into varying lengths—approximately 12in/30.5cm to 36in/92cm long. Cut the double-knitting-weight yarn to twice this length. Fold the double-knitting weight yarns in half so that they are double (see the Special Yarn Note, above), then knot the lengths together, end to end, introducing the colors randomly. (To reduce the number of knots, you can link the doubled yarn together at the fold where possible.)

Note: When you are knitting, try to position the knots on the wrong side of the work. If the occasional knot does pop through onto the right side, it is easy to push it back to the wrong side when you reach it on the next row.

BASE PIECES (MAKE 2)

With size 9 (5.5mm) needles and prepared yarn, cast on 88 (100: 112) sts.
Mark 14th (20th: 26th) cast-on st and 74th (80th: 86th) cast-on st with a colored thread to show position of opening on base of beanbag.
Work 20 rows in garter st (knit every row).
Cont in garter st throughout, dec 1 st at each end of next row and then at each end of every foll alt row 28 (30: 32) times in all. (*32 (40: 48) sts.*)
Dec 1 st at each end of next 6 (10: 14) rows.
Bind off rem 20 sts knitwise.
Make second base piece in same way.

TOP SEGMENTS (MAKE 4)

With size 9 (5.5mm) needles, cast on 74 (80: 86) sts.
Work 40 (70: 100) rows in garter st (knit every row).
Cont in garter st throughout, dec 1 st at each end of next row and then at each end of every foll 3rd row 26 (29: 32) times in all. (*22 sts.*)
Next row *K2tog, k3; rep from * to last 2 sts, k2tog. (*17 sts.*)
Work 2 rows in garter st.
Next row *K2tog, k2; rep from * to last 5 sts, k2tog, k1, k2tog. (*12 sts.*)
Work 2 rows in garter st.
Next row K2tog, k1, [k2tog] 3 times, k1, k2tog. (*7 sts.*)
Work 2 rows in garter st.
Next row K2tog, k3tog, k2tog. (*3 sts.*)
Work 1 row in garter st.
Next row K3tog, break off yarn, thread tail end through rem st, and pull tight to fasten off.

TO FINISH

Darn in all yarn ends and push all knots on right side through to wrong side.
Press all pieces lightly on wrong side, following instructions on yarn label.
Using a single strand of a double-knitting-weight yarn, sew pieces together as follows:
With right sides together, sew two base pieces together along cast-on edges, stitching from side edges to markers (leaving a large opening between markers for inserting cushion). Remove markers.
Sew together four top segments, stitching from tips (which are at center of cover) to cast-on edge.
Sew cast-on edge of top to base, aligning seams on base with two of segment seams.
Sew four large snaps, equally spaced apart, to opening.

BEANBAG CUSHION

PAPER PATTERN PIECES

Use newspaper or other large sheets of paper to make the paper pattern for the cushion. (The cushion is circular, and once inserted in the knitted cover, it gives the beanbag its circular shape.)

Pattern piece for circular base

Cut a paper rectangle $11\frac{1}{2}$ (13: $14\frac{1}{2}$) in/ 29 (33: 36.5)cm by 23 (26: 29)in/ 58 (66: 73)cm.

Fold the rectangle in half to make a square. Using a homemade compass and measuring from one of the corners at the fold, mark $11\frac{1}{2}$ (13: $14\frac{1}{2}$)in/29 (33: 36.5)cm from this corner and in a curve from the adjacent corner across the square to the opposite corner. Keeping the paper folded, cut along the marked curve, then open out the semicircle. (This finished pattern piece includes the seam allowance along the curved edge, but not along the straight edge.) Mark the position for the 18in/45cm zipper at the center of the straight edge of the semicircle.

Pattern piece for top segments

Cut a paper rectangle 18 ($20\frac{1}{2}$: 23)in/ 46 (52: 58)cm by 17 (22: 27)in/ 43 (55.5: 68.5)cm.

Then shape this rectangle into the shape of one of the four top segments of the cushion as follows:

Lay the rectangle with an edge 18 (20.5: 23)in/46 (52: 58)cm long at the bottom— this edge is the base of the segment. Measure up from the base 5 (7: 9)in/ 12.5 (17.5: 22.5)cm along both the right and left side edge of the rectangle and make a mark.

Find the center of the top edge of the rectangle (you can fold the rectangle in half to find the center) and mark. Then draw a gentle curve from the center of the top of the rectangle to each of the marks made at the side edges.

Cut along the curves. (This finished pattern piece does not include seam allowances.)

TO CUT FABRIC PIECES

Using the pattern for the circular base, cut two base pieces from the fabric, adding an extra $\frac{1}{2}$in/1.5cm along the straight edge of the paper pattern for the seam allowance at the center of the cushion. Mark the position for the zipper on each of these pieces. Using the pattern for the top segments, cut four top segments from the fabric, adding an extra $\frac{1}{2}$in/1.5cm all around the paper pattern for the seam allowance.

TO SEW THE CUSHION

Pin the two base pieces together along the straight edges, with right sides together. Taking a $\frac{1}{2}$in/1.5cm seam allowance throughout, stitch the seam, leaving a 18in/45cm opening for the zipper as

marked. Press the seam open and press $\frac{1}{2}$in/1.5cm to the wrong side along the zipper opening. Stitch the zipper in place and set the cushion base aside.

With right sides together, pin two top segments together along one curved edge, and stitch. Stitch the two remaining top segments together in the same way. Pin the two halves of the top together and stitch, to make a large cone shape.

Open the zipper, then pin the cone-shaped top to the base, with right sides together and aligning the base seams with two of the top segments seams (ease in the top as necessary to fit the base). Stitch along this seam twice (for strength).

Clip the seam allowances around the curves as necessary, so that the seams lie flat. Press.

Turn right side out. Fill the cushion with polystyrene balls until it is about one third full and zipper the opening closed.

Insert the cushion in the knitted beanbag cover and snap closed.

ANTI-FIREWORKS **DOG** BALACLAVA

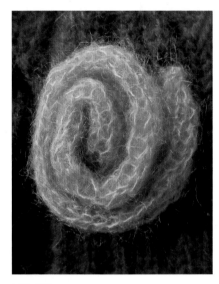

LEVEL
Easy

SIZES
Small—to fit small to medium-size dog
The finished small size measures
approximately 9¹/₂in/24cm around
the neck and 10¹/₂in/26.5cm long
unstretched.
Large—to fit medium-size to large dog
The finished large size measures
approximately 12¹/₂in/32cm around
the neck and 12in/30.5cm long
unstretched.
Note: The ribbed balaclava is stretchy
and will fit easily over the dog's head;
when on the dog, the circumference
will be wider and the length shorter
than when unstretched.

MATERIALS
Aran/Medium Weight Yarn (CYCA 4),
approx. 153 (306) yds in main color
MC for balaclava (shown in *Rowan
Kid Classic*)
Small amount of Lace Weight Yarn
in contrasting color **A**, for earmuffs
(shown in *Rowan Kidsilk Haze*)
Pair of size 8 (5mm) knitting needles

GAUGE
18–19 sts and 23–25 rows to
4in/10cm measured over St st
using size 8 (5mm) knitting needles
and MC.

ABBREVIATIONS
See page 30.

TO MAKE BALACLAVA
With size 8 (5mm) needles and MC,
cast on 62 (82) sts.
Beg k2, p2 rib as follows:
1st rib row (RS) *K2, p2; rep from * to
last 2 sts, k2.
2nd rib row *P2, k2; rep from * to last
2 sts, p2.
(Last 2 rows are repeated to form k2,
p2 rib patt.)
Work 38 (44) rows more in k2, p2 rib,
ending with a WS row.

Divide for front opening
Keeping rib patt correct as set, divide for
opening on next row as follows:
Next row (RS) Work first 25 (32) sts in
rib and slip these sts onto a st holder, then
bind off next 12 (18) sts in rib, work in
rib to end.
Working on these 25 (32) sts only, cont
as follows:
Work 15 (19) rows in rib, ending with
a WS row.
Break off MC and leave these sts on
a spare needle.
With WS facing, rejoin MC to sts on
holder and work in rib to end.
Work 14 (18) rows in rib, ending with
a WS row.
Next row (RS) Work in rib across 25 (32)
on needle, cast on 12 (18) sts onto right-
hand needle, then work in rib across 25
(32) sts on spare needle. *(62 (82) sts.)*
Work 1 row in rib.

Shape top
Next row (RS) *K6, k2tog; rep from * to
last 6 (2) sts, k6 (2). *(55 (72) sts.)*

Purl 1 row.
Next row *K5, k2tog; rep from * to last
6 (2) sts, k6 (2). *(48 (62) sts.)*
Purl 1 row.
Next row *K4, k2tog; rep from * to last
6 (2) sts, k6 (2). *(41 (52) sts.)*
Purl 1 row.
Next row *K3, k2tog; rep from * to last
6 (2) sts, k6 (2). *(34 (42) sts.)*
Purl 1 row.
Next row *K2, k2tog; rep from * to last
6 (2) sts, k6 (2). *(27 (32) sts.)*
Purl 1 row.
Next row [K2tog] 13 (16) times, k1 (0).
(14 (16) sts.)
Next row [P2tog] 7 (8) times. *(7 (8) sts.)*
Next row [K2tog] 3 (4) times, k1 (0).
(4 sts.)
Next row [P2tog] twice. *(2 sts.)*
Next row K2tog, then break off MC,
thread tail end through rem st, and pull
tight to fasten off.

EARMUFFS (MAKE 2)
With size 8 (5mm) needles and A, cast on
10 sts.
Beg with a k row, work in St st until strip
measures 10in/25cm from cast-on edge,
ending with a WS row.
Bind off, leaving a long tail end.

TO FINISH
Press balaclava very lightly on WS,
following instructions on yarn label.
Sew side edges of balaclava together
to form back seam.

Earmuffs
Do not press earmuff strips, but allow them
to curl in along side edges to form a long
tube shape. Starting at cast-on end, curl
each strip into a spiraling circle (like a
snail), about 2¹/₂in/6.5cm in diameter.
Thread long tail end onto a blunt-ended
yarn needle and secure circle shape by
passing needle through circle spirals from
one edge of circle to opposite edge.
Sew one earmuff to each side of balaclava,
level with center of front opening.

RUFFLE **DOG** COLLAR

LEVEL
Easy

SIZES
The finished collar cover measures approximately 1¹/₂in/4cm wide for all sizes, and the lengths are as follows:
Extra-extra small—to fit collar size 10in/25cm
Extra small—to fit collar size 12in/30.5cm
Small—to fit collar size 14in/35.5cm
Medium—to fit collar size 16in/40.5cm
Large—to fit collar size 18in/45.5cm
Extra large—to fit collar size 20in/50.5cm

MATERIALS
Fingering/Super Fine Weight Yarn (CYCA 1), approx. 200 yds (200: 400: 400: 400: 400) in main color **MC** (shown in *Jaeger Matchmaker Merino 4-Ply*)
Lace Weight Yarn, approx. 229 yds in contrasting color **A** (shown in *Rowan Kidsilk Haze*)
Pair of size 3 (3.25mm) knitting needles

GAUGE
28 sts and 36 rows to 4in/10cm measured over St st using size 3 (3.25mm) needles and MC.

ABBREVIATIONS
See page 30.

TO MAKE COLLAR COVER
With size 3 (3.25mm) needles and MC, cast on 24 sts.
Work 2 rows in garter st (knit every row).
Beg St st section as follows:
1st row (RS) K6, p1, k17.
2nd row P17, k1, p6.
Rep last 2 rows until collar cover measures 9 (11: 13: 15: 17: 19)in/22.5 (28: 33: 38: 43: 48)cm from cast-on edge, ending with a WS row.
Work 2 rows in garter st, ending with a WS row.
Next row (RS) Bind off first 12 sts knitwise, k to end. *(12 sts.)*
Work 10 rows in garter st.
Bind off knitwise.

RUFFLE
With size 3 (3.25mm) needles and A, cast on 165 (195: 231: 267: 306: 363) sts.
Work 2 rows in garter st (knit every row).
Break off A, change to MC, and cont as follows:
Work 12 rows in garter st.
Next row *K3tog; rep from * to end. *(55 (65: 77: 89: 102: 121) sts.)*
Work 2 rows in garter st.
Next row [K1, p1, k1] all into each st to end (to inc twice into each st). *(165 (195: 231: 267: 306: 363) sts.)*
Work 12 rows in garter st.
Break off MC, change to A, and cont as follows:

Work 2 rows in garter st.
Bind off knitwise.

TO FINISH
Press collar cover lightly on wrong side, following instructions on yarn label.
With wrong side of ruffle facing right side of collar cover, sew ruffle to collar cover, stitching along center of ruffle and through line of rev St st on collar cover.
Fold collar cover in half lengthwise and sew long side edges together to form a tube.
Sew bound-off edge of collar cover to corresponding section of cast-on edge.
Slip cover onto dog's collar, positioning buckle over garter st section.

PARAKEET BLANKET

LEVEL
Intermediate

SIZE
The finished blanket measures approximately 23¹/₄in/59cm wide by 54in/137cm long.
Note: To make the blanket longer, you can add rows in MC before beginning the chart and the same number of rows in MC after completing the chart. To make the blanket wider, add the same number of stitches to each side of chart in MC.

MATERIALS
Light/DK Weight Yarn (CYCA 3), approx. 650 yds in main color **MC** (dark olive), for borders and outer background (shown in *Jaeger Matchmaker Merino DK*)
Approx. 390 yds of same yarn in **E** (pale blue), for center background
Approx. 130 yds in each of 5 different colors **A** (mid green), **B** (pale lime green), **C** (light green), **D** (dark green), and **F** (brown), for leaf motifs
Pair of size 6 (4mm) knitting needles

GAUGE
22 sts and 30 rows to 4in/10cm measured over St st using size 6 (4mm) needles.

ABBREVIATIONS
See page 30.

CHART NOTE
The chart is worked in St st. When working from the chart, read odd-numbered rows (k rows) from right to left, and even-numbered rows (p rows) from left to right. When working the chart pattern, use the intarsia method, knitting with a separate small ball (or long length) of yarn for each area of color and twisting yarns together on wrong side when changing color to avoid holes.
Note: The chart shows only the St st section of the blanket; the garter stitch borders are not included on the chart.
Note 2: Despite its name, this project works well for all sorts of feathered pets—from shy lovebirds to cheeky cockatiels like the fellow pictured above.

TO MAKE BLANKET
With size 6 (4mm) needles and MC, cast on 130 sts.
Work 10 rows in garter st (knit every row). Beg St st patt with garter st borders for center of cover as follows:
Next row (RS) Knit.
Next row K10, p110, k10.
Rep last 2 rows 18 times more, ending with a WS row.
Set position of chart patt (see pages 28–29) on next 2 rows as follows:
Next row (RS) K10; k next 110 sts foll chart row 1; k10.
Next row K10; p next 110 sts foll chart row 2; k10.
Cont foll chart as set and working 10-st garter st borders until all 162 rows of chart have been completed, ending with a WS row.
Then turn chart upside down and cont in patt by working all 162 rows in opposite direction—a total of 324 chart rows in total, ending with a WS row.
Using MC only for remainder of cover, work 38 rows in St st with 10-st garter st borders.
Work 10 rows in garter st.
Bind off knitwise.

TO FINISH
Block and press cover lightly on wrong side, following instructions on yarn label and avoiding garter st borders.

LEVEL
Easy

SIZE
The finished water lily measures approximately 4–4³/₄in/10–12cm in diameter and each leaf measures approximately 3¹/₂–4in/9–10cm in length.

MATERIALS
One green plastic bag, to make "yarn" **A** for leaves
One white or pink plastic bag, to make "yarn" **B** for petals
One orange plastic bag, to make "yarn" **C** for stamens
Pair of size 6 (4mm) knitting needles
Matching sewing thread, for sewing together petals and sewing on stamens

GAUGE
It is not necessary to knit to a specific gauge to make the water lily. The size will vary (see Size above) according to the thickness of the plastic used for the "yarn," the width of the plastic strips, and the knitter's individual tension.

ABBREVIATIONS
See page 30.

SPECIAL NOTE
The plastic "yarn" is knitted in garter stitch (knit every row) in the usual way. The "yarn" will stretch while you are knitting with it, so be careful not to pull it too tightly because this might break it, and the more breaks the more knots and the more tails ends you will have to darn in later.

TO PREPARE PLASTIC "YARN"
Using scissors, cut off the bottom and handles of each bag (including gusset), so that it forms a large tube.
Cut each bag into a continuous "yarn" strip as follows:
Open out bag. Then starting at the bottom of bag, cut a continuous strip of plastic in a spiral (as you would peel an apple), about ³/₈in/1cm wide. If the bag has printing on it, you can either cut out that section or incorporate into your knitting "yarn." Loosely wind the strip into a ball as you proceed.

If the plastic breaks while you are preparing it, just knot the strips together.

LEAVES (MAKE 2)
With size 6 (4mm) needles and A, cast on 4 sts.
Knit 1 row.
Cont in garter st throughout, inc 1 st at each end of next row 5 rows. (*14 sts.*)
Knit 1 row.
Inc 1 st at each end of next row. (*16 sts.*)
Work even in garter st for 10 rows.

Divide leaf
Before beg next row to divide leaf, mark this side of work as RS, using a colored thread.
Next row (RS) K8, then turn, leaving rem sts on a st holder.
Working on these 8 sts only, cont as follows:
Knit 1 row.
Dec 1 st at beg of next row (outer leaf edge). (*7 sts.*)

Knit 1 row.
Dec 1 st at beg of next row. (*6 sts.*)
Dec 1 st at outer leaf edge on each of next 4 rows. (*2 sts.*)
Bind off.
With RS facing, rejoin A to 8 sts on holder leaving a tail end 8in/20cm long (for attaching leaves to flowers), then k to end.
Knit 1 row.
Dec 1 st at end of next row (outer leaf edge). (*7 sts.*)
Knit 1 row.
Dec 1 st at end of next row. (*6 sts.*)
Dec 1 st at outer leaf edge on each of next 4 rows. (*2 sts.*)
Bind off.
Make 1 more leaf in same way.

SMALL INNER PETALS (MAKE 5)
With size 6 (4mm) needles and B, cast on 5 sts.
Knit 1 row.
Cont in garter st throughout, inc 1 st at

each end of next row. (*7 sts.*)
Work even in garter st for 8 rows.
Dec 1 st at each end of next 2 rows. (*3 sts.*)
Next row K2tog, k1.
Next row K2tog, then break off B, thread tail end through rem st, and pull to fasten off.
Make 4 more inner petals in same way.

LARGE OUTER PETALS (MAKE 5)
With size 6 (4mm) needles and B, cast on 7 sts.
Knit 1 row.
Cont in garter st throughout, inc 1 st at each end of next row. (*9 sts.*)
Knit 1 row.
Inc 1 st at each end of next row. (*11 sts.*)
Work even in garter st for 8 rows.
Dec 1 st at each end of next 4 rows. (*3 sts.*)
Next row K2tog, k1.
Next row K2tog, then break off B, thread

tail end through rem st, and pull to fasten off.
Make 4 more outer petals in same way, leaving a 8in/20cm tail end on 2 of them when casting on, to attach flowers to leaves.

STAMENS (MAKE 3)
With size 6 (4mm) needles and C, cast on 8 sts.
Bind off.
Make 2 more stamens in same way.

TO FINISH
Darn in ends of plastic "yarn," but leave ends left long on purpose (on leaves and two of large outer petals).
Take two large petals and overlap them so that one is on top of half of the other, with cast-on edges aligned. Using a sewing needle and matching thread, sew these two petals together along cast-on edge,

slightly gathering base of petals. Continue sewing on remaining three large petals to first two in same way, overlapping each added petal and slightly gathering along base to form a ring of petals. (Leave two long tail ends at back of flower.)
Sew together five small petals in same way to make a ring, then sew to center of ring of large petals.
Sew three stamens to center of water lily, using matching sewing thread, and secure thread to back of flower. Pull petals upward to make water lily look realistic.
Underneath flower, knot together two long tail ends from flower and two from leaves, about 1in/2.5cm away from flowers and leaves. Then to form a trailing "root," braid together these tail ends (using two flower tail ends as one strand) and knot together at end. Trim ends close to knot.

TORTOISE HIBERNATION TENT

LEVEL

Knitted tent: Easy
Wooden tent frame: Intermediate

SIZE

The finished tent measures approximately 14in/35cm wide by 19in/48cm long by 15in/37.5cm tall.

MATERIALS

Knitted tent

Light/DK Weight (CYCA 3), approx. 260 yds in **A** (mid blue), for base of tent (shown in *Jaeger Matchmaker Merino DK*)
Approx. 260 yds of same yarn in **B** (lilac), for one side of tent
Approx. 260 yds of same yarn in **C** (light sea blue), for one side of tent
Approx. 130 yds of same yarn in **D** (dark green), for back of tent
Approx. 130 yds of same yarn in **E** (light green), for front of tent
Pair of size 6 (4mm) knitting needles

Wooden tent frame

3 lengths of wooden doweling, each ¹/₄in/6mm in diameter and approximately 51cm/20in long (to fit along two sides of base of tent and along top of tent)
2 lengths of wooden doweling, each ¹/₄in/6mm in diameter and approximately 40.5cm/16in long (to fit along front and back of base of tent)
4 lengths of wooden doweling, each ¹/₄in/6mm in diameter and approximately 48.5cm/19in long (to form A-shape frames at front and back of tent)
Jute twine or string (a slightly rough version will hold better)
Strong adhesive tape, for binding frame joints

GAUGE

22 sts and 30 rows to 4in/10cm measured over St st using size 6 (4mm) needles.

ABBREVIATIONS

See page 30.

SPECIAL NOTE

Do not cut the doweling into pieces for the frame until you have finished knitting the tent. Because of variable gauges you may need to adjust the length of the wooden rods to fit the size of the finished knitting.

KNITTED TENT

BASE OF TENT

With size 6 (4mm) needles and A, cast on 106 sts.

1st row (RS) K to end.
2nd row K5, p to end.

Rep last 2 rows (working in St st with a 5-st border in garter st along tent front edge as set) until base measures 14in/35cm from cast-on edge (approximately 104 rows in total), ending with a p row.
Bind off.

LONG SIDE OF TENT (MAKE 2)

With size 6 (4mm) needles and B, cast on 106 sts.

Beg with a k row, work in St st until side measures 15in/37.5cm from cast-on edge (approximately 112 rows in total), ending with a p row.
Bind off.
Make second side in same way, but using C.

BACK OF TENT

With size 6 (4mm) needles and D, cast on 80 sts.

Beg with a k row, work 2 rows in St st, ending with a p row.

Cont in St st throughout, dec 1 st at each end of next row and then at each end of every foll 3rd row until 2 sts rem (118 rows in total), ending with a p row.

Next row K2tog, then break off D, thread tail end through rem st, and pull tight to fasten off.

RIGHT FRONT OF TENT

With size 6 (4mm) needles and E, cast on 41 sts.

Work 2 rows in garter st (knit every row).
Cont in garter st, dec 1 st at beg of next row. *(39 sts.)*

Work 1 row more in garter st.
Next row (RS) K to end.
Next row K5, p to last 2 sts, p2tog. *(37 sts.)*
Next row K to end.
Next row K5, p to end.

Cont as set, working in St st with a 5-st border in garter st along left edge, **and at the same time** dec 1 st at beg of next row and at same edge (edge without border) on every foll 3rd row until 2 sts rem, ending with a p row.

Next row K2tog, then break off E, thread tail end through rem st, and pull tight to fasten off.

LEFT FRONT OF TENT

With size 6 (4mm) needles and E, cast on 41 sts.

Work 2 rows in garter st (knit every row).
Cont in garter st, dec 1 st at end of next row. *(39 sts.)*

Work 1 row more in garter st.
Next row (RS) K to end.
Next row P2tog, p to last 5 sts, k5. *(37 sts.)*
Next row K to end.
Next row P to last 5 sts, k5.

Cont as set, working in St st with a 5-st border in garter st along right edge, **and at the same time** dec 1 st at end of next row and at same edge (edge without border) on every foll 3rd row until 2 sts rem, ending with a p row.

Next row K2tog, then break off E, thread tail end through rem st, and pull tight to fasten off.

FLAGS

With size 6 (4mm) needles and A, cast on 116 sts.
Knit 1 row.

Next row (RS) Bind off first 19 sts knitwise, k until there are 8 sts on right needle, then turn, leaving rem sts unworked.
Working on these 8 sts only, drop A and make first flag as follows:

**Using B for flag, work 7 rows in garter st (knit every row).

Cont in garter st for flag throughout, dec 1 st at each end of next row. *(6 sts.)*
Work 7 rows in garter st.
Dec 1 st at each end of next row. *(4 sts.)*
Work 7 rows in garter st.
Next row [K2tog] twice. *(2 sts.)*
Work 1 row in garter st.
Next row K2tog, then break off flag yarn, thread tail end through rem st, and pull tight to fasten off.**

*****With RS facing, return to sts left unworked and using A, bind off 2 sts knitwise, k until there are 8 sts on right needle, then turn, leaving rem sts unworked. Working on these 8 sts only, drop A and make next flag as for first flag from ** to ** but using C.*****

Rep from ***** to ***** 6 times more, using D for 3rd flag, E for 4th flag, B for 5th flag, C for 6th flag, D for 7th flag, and E for 8th flag.

With RS facing, return to sts left unworked and using A, bind off rem sts knitwise.

TO FINISH

Block and press tent pieces lightly on wrong side, following instructions on yarn label.

With right sides together, sew cast-on edge of tent base to cast-on edge of side worked in B, and sew bound-off edge of tent base to cast-on edge of side worked in C. Then sew bound-off edges of sides together at top to form a triangular shape.

Sew back of tent to back of base (end without garter st border) and sides, leaving a 1in/2.5cm opening at top for wooden rod to stick out of.

Sew fronts together for 1in/2.5cm at center top, 1in/2.5cm below top edge, so leaving a split at apex for rod.

Cords

Make six cords as follows:
Using E, cut two strands of yarn each 14¾in/37.5cm long. Holding two strands together, knot each end. Ask a friend to hold one end (or tie one end to a door handle). Insert a pencil in front of knot between two strands at each end and have person at each end twist pencil clockwise until strands are very tightly twisted. Fold twisted yarn in half, give it a slight pull, then allow it to twist up on itself. Smooth out any unevenness, working away from knots. Knot together knotted end, and cut off original two knots. Sew folded (unknotted) end of each cord to center of borders on tent fronts, stitching three to each front and spacing them evenly apart.

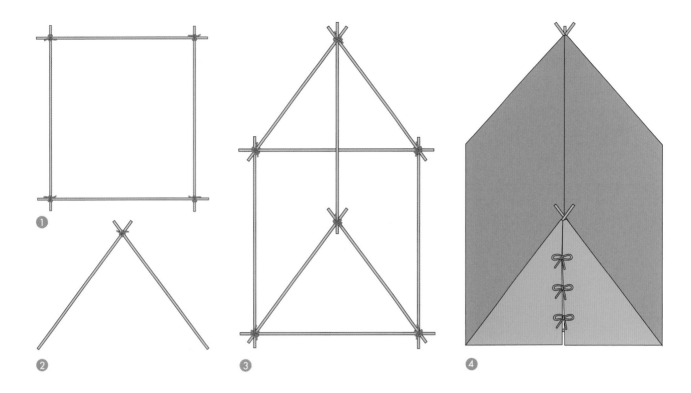

WOODEN TENT FRAME

TO CUT FRAME PIECES

Check that the tent width, length, and height match the sizes given at the beginning of the pattern, and adjust the doweling lengths given in the Materials list if necessary.

Next, cut nine doweling pieces to the correct lengths with a saw, and gently sand the ends.

TO ASSEMBLE FRAME

Cut the twine into 12in/30.5cm lengths. **(Fig 1)** Starting with the base-frame of the tent, use twine to bind together two 20in/51cm lengths of doweling (to fit along the sides of the tent base) with two 16in/40.5cm lengths (to fit along the front and back of the tent base). To bind the rods together, wrap the twine over

and around the "joint," leaving about 1/2in/12mm of the rods protruding. Once the joint is fairly secure, knot the twine. (When the tent is finished, the structure will be more stable.)

(Fig 2) Take two 19in/48.5cm lengths of doweling and bind them together at the top to form an A-shape for the back of the tent, leaving about 2in/5cm above the binding (as on a wigwam) to tie the flags onto.

(Fig 3) Place the bottom of the A-shape on the inside of the back corners of the base-frame and bind in place with twine. Make a second A-shape frame for the front of the tent, using the remaining two 19in/48.5cm lengths of doweling; then bind it to the base-frame.

Wrap the tape around the four joints at the base of the tent to stop the rods from sliding.

Rest the remaining 20in/51cm length of doweling in the crosses at the top of A-shapes, and bind in place at each end using twine only.

TO SET UP TENT

(Fig 4) Carefully slip the tent over the frame, allowing the crossed points of doweling to pass through the openings at the two top corners of the tent.

To secure the flags to the tent, tie one end to the top of left front rod and tie the other end to right back rod.

Fill the tent with straw and introduce your tortoise.

CARROT CURTAIN

LEVEL
Intermediate

SIZE
The finished carrot curtain measures approximately 14in/35.5cm wide by 12¹/₂in/32cm long.

Note: The curtain can be made wider or longer to fit your hutch by adding more stitches or rows.

MATERIALS
DK/Medium Weight Yarn (CYCA 4), approx. 272 yds in **MC** (dark gray), for background (shown in *Rowan Pure Wool DK*)

Approx. 136 yds of same yarn in **A** (orange) for carrots

Lace Weight Yarn approx. 229 yds in **B** (green) for carrot stalks (shown in *Rowan Kidsilk Haze*)

Pair of size 6 (4mm) knitting needles

Wooden dowel, 17in/43cm long by ¹/₄in/6mm in diameter, for curtain pole

2 metal screw-in hooks, for attaching dowel to front of hutch

GAUGE
22 sts and 30 rows to 4in/10cm measured over St st using size 6 (4mm) needles and MC.

ABBREVIATIONS
See page 30.

CHART NOTE
The background in the center of the curtain is worked in reverse stockinette stitch and the carrot motifs in stockinette stitch. There is a 5-stitch seed stitch border along each side edge of the curtain center to form firm edges.

When working from the chart, read odd-numbered rows (right-side rows) from right to left, and even-numbered rows (wrong-side rows) from left to right.

When working the carrot motifs, use the intarsia method, knitting with a separate small ball (or long length) of yarn for each area of color and twisting yarns together on wrong side when changing color to avoid holes.

The carrot stalks are knitted separately and sewn onto the completed curtain.

TO MAKE CURTAIN
With size 6 (4mm) needles and MC, cast on 83 sts.

Work lower border in seed st as follows:

1st seed st row (RS) K1, *p1, k1; rep from * to end.

(Last row is repeated to form seed st.)

Work 9 rows more in seed st, ending with a WS row.

Set patt for center as follows:

1st patt row (RS) K1, [p1, k1] twice, p to last 5 sts, [k1, p1] twice, k1.

2nd patt row K1, [p1, k1] twice, K to last 5 sts, [k1, p1] twice, k1.

Rep last 2 rows once more, ending with a WS row.

Using MC and A as required, position carrot motifs (see page 30) on next 2 rows (chart rows 5 and 6) as follows:

Next row (RS) Using MC k1, [p1, k1] twice, p8, *using A k1, using MC p13; rep from * 3 times more, using A k1, using MC p8, [k1, p1] twice, k1.

Next row Using MC k1, [p1, k1] twice, k8, *using A p1, using MC k13; rep from * 3 times more, using A p1, using MC k8, [k1, p1] twice, k1.

Cont as set, keeping 5-st side borders in seed st and following chart for 73 center sts (working carrot motifs in St st and A, and background in rev St st and MC) until all 78 chart rows have been completed, ending with a WS row.

Break off A.

Rep 1st and 2nd patt rows 5 times, ending with a WS row.

Next row (RS) Rep 2nd patt row (to form a p-st ridge on WS).

Rep 2nd patt row once more.

Rep 1st and 2nd patt rows 4 times more. Bind off in patt.

CARROT STALKS (MAKE 14)
With size 6 (4mm) needles and B, cast on 15 sts.

Bind off 15 sts knitwise.

Make 13 more carrot stalks in same way.

TO FINISH
Block and press curtain lightly on wrong side, following instructions on yarn label. Fold each stalk into a V-shape as shown, and sew one to top of each of 14 carrot motifs on curtain, using B.

Fold bound-off edge at top of curtain to wrong side and slip stitch bound-off edge to ridge row to form a channel at top of curtain. Insert curtain pole into channel. Screw two metal hooks to hutch, and slide curtain pole in place on hooks.

PET ROSETTE

LEVEL
Easy

SIZE
The finished rosette with pleated border measures approximately 4³/₄in/12cm in diameter and the tails measure approximately 5in/12.5cm and 6in/15.5cm long.

MATERIALS
DK/Medium Weight Yarn (CYCA 4), approx. 136 in **MC** (dark gray), for rosette (shown in *Rowan Pure Wool DK*)
Small amount of same yarn in contrasting color **A** for edging
Pair of size 6 (4mm) knitting needles
Small piece of cardboard, to stiffen rosette center
Safety pin

GAUGE
22 sts and 30 rows to 4in/10cm measured over St st using size 6 (4mm) needles.

ABBREVIATIONS
See page 30.

ROSETTE CENTER
With size 6 (4mm) needles and MC, cast on 10 sts.
Beg with a k row, work 2 rows in St st, ending with a p row.
Cont in St st throughout, inc 1 st at each end of next row and then at each end of 3 foll alt rows, ending with a k row. *(18 sts.)*
Work even in St st for 10 rows, ending with a k row.
Dec 1 st at each end of next row and then at each end of 3 foll alt rows, ending with a p row. *(10 sts.)*
Work even for 2 rows. Bind off.

PLEAT STRIP
With size 6 (4mm) needles and MC, cast on 120 sts.

For pleat with plain edging only
Beg with a k row, work 8 rows in St st, ending with a p (WS) row.

For pleat with a seeded edging only
Beg with a k row, work 7 rows in St st, ending with a k (RS) row.

For both versions
Break off MC and change to A.
Knit 1 row.
Bind off knitwise.

SHORT TAIL
With size 6 (4mm) needles and MC, cast on 8 sts. Work in garter st (knit every row) until tail measures 4in/10cm from cast-on edge.
∗∗Divide tail
Before beg next row to divide tail, mark this side of work as RS, using a colored thread.

Next row (RS) K4, then turn, leaving rem sts on a st holder.
Working on these 4 sts only, cont as follows:
Next row (WS) K2tog, k2. *(3 sts.)*
Knit 1 row.
Next row K2tog, k1. *(2 sts.)*
Knit 1 row.
Next row K2tog, then break off MC, thread tail end through rem st, and pull tight to fasten off.
With RS facing, rejoin MC to 4 sts on st holder and k to end.
Next row (WS) K2, k2tog. *(3 sts.)*
Knit 1 row
Next row K1, k2tog. *(2 sts.)*
Knit 1 row.
Next row K2tog, then break off MC, thread tail end through rem st, and pull tight to fasten off.

LONG TAIL
With size 6 (4mm) needles and MC, cast on 8 sts.
Work in garter st (knit every row) until tail measures 6in/15cm from cast-on edge.
Complete as for short tail from ∗∗.

TO FINISH
Do not press.
Cut a circle of cardboard 2³/₈in/6cm in diameter. Place cardboard circle on wrong side of knitted rosette center. Then using a blunt-ended yarn needle and a strand of MC, weave yarn in and out around edge of rosette center; pull tight to gather edge and enclose cardboard inside knitting, and fasten off. Using MC, sew safety pin to back of rosette center (over top of gathered edge).

Pleated border
Fold pleat strip into approximately 4-stitch pleats along cast-on edge (so that it will fit around rosette center), and sew pleats in place using MC. Using mattress stitch, sew ends of pleated strip together to form a ring. Sew pleated ring to back of rosette center, close to edge. Sew cast-on ends of tails (one on top of the other and with short tail to front) to wrong side of lower edge of rosette center.

Parakeet Blanket
Chart (page 16)

KEY
MC A B C D E F

Carrot Curtain
Chart
(page 24)

KEY

■ p on RS and k on
WS, using **MC**

▨ k on RS and p on
WS, using **A**

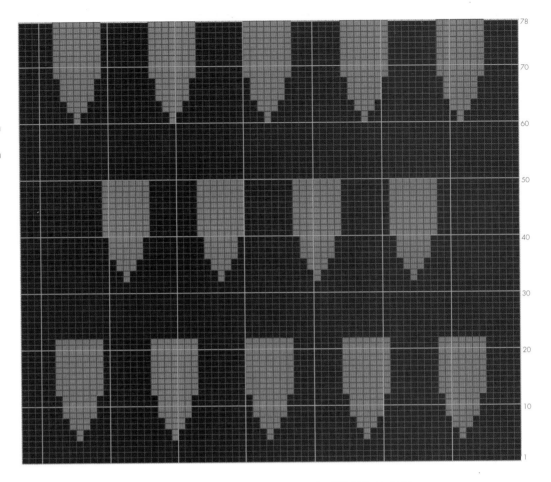

```
                                                                    78

                                                                    70



                                                                    60



                                                                    50



                                                                    40


                                                                    30



                                                                    20



                                                                    10


                                                                    1
```

A B B R E V I A T I O N S

The following are the abbreviations used in this book.
Special abbreviations are given with individual patterns.

alt	alternate
beg	begin(ning)
cm	centimeter(s)
cont	continu(e)(ing)
dec	decreas(e)(ing)
DK	double knitting (a lightweight yarn)
foll	follow(s)(ing)
g	gram(s)
in	inch(es)
inc	increas(e)(ing)
k	knit
k2tog	knit next 2 sts together
m	meter(s)
MC	main color (of yarn)
mm	millimeter(s)
oz	ounce(s)
p	purl
p2tog	purl next 2 sts together
patt	pattern

psso	pass slipped stitch over
rem	remain(s)(ing)
rep	repeat(s)(ing)
rev St st	reverse stockinette stitch; purl sts on RS rows and knit sts on WS rows
RS	right side
sl	slip
st(s)	stitch(es)
St st	stockinette stitch; knit sts on RS rows and purl sts on WS rows
tbl	through back loop(s)
tog	together
WS	wrong side
yo	yarn over (yarn over right-hand needle to make a new stitch)
*	Repeat instructions after asterisk or between asterisks as many times as instructed.
[ ]	Repeat instructions inside square brackets as many times as instructed
-	Where a hyphen appears instead of a number, it means that instructions do not apply to that size

KNITTING FOR PETS

YARN SPECIFICS

The accessories in this book have been designed using Rowan and Jaeger Yarns, which are widely available throughout the United States, Europe, and over the Internet. Visit www.knitrowan.com where you will find a full range of yarns, colors, and suppliers. If you are a beginner, you can go to a local yarn store where the helpful staff will give you all the assistance you need to track down yarns.

The majority of these pet accessories are knitted in double-knitting-weight wool yarns. If you decide to use a yarn other than the specified yarn, do remember to knit a 4in (10cm) square to check the gauge and then adjust the needle size accordingly.

The number of yards (meters) per 1^3/$_4$oz (50g) ball varies from yarn to yarn, so when using a substitute yarn, be sure to calculate the number of balls you need by the number of yards (meters) rather than by weight.

Some of the designs use small amounts of several colors. These give you the opportunity to use up leftover yarns. Before beginning, however, check the yarn descriptions to make sure that your leftovers are a good match in thickness to the main color you are using.

GAUGE

Working your knitting to the correct size can be important, especially for larger knits, so be sure to knit a gauge swatch. Count the number of stitches and rows to 4in (10cm) on your swatch. If your swatch has more rows or stitches than the number specified, then use knitting needles that are one size larger, and if it has fewer stitches or rows, then try one size smaller needles. Getting the number of stitches to 4in (10cm) right is more important than the number of rows, as length is generally determined by merely knitting to a specified length in inches (centimeters).

Working a gauge swatch sounds tedious, but it is definitely worth the time it takes, particularly if the design comes in various sizes. The swatch also gives you a chance to see how the yarn and stitch pattern knit up. Keep these swatches, and once you have collected about 20, sew them together into a blanket for your pet

PROTECT YOUR PETS

The most essential thing to remember when knitting for your pets is to make sure that all beads and buttons are securely sewn on—you don't want your animals to swallow them.

STANDARD YARN WEIGHT CHART

Yarn Weight Symbol and Category Name	Super Fine 1	Fine 2	Light 3	Medium 4	Bulky 5	Super Bulky 6
Types of yarn in category	Sock, fingering, baby	Sport, baby	DK, light worsted	Worsted, afghan, Aran	Chunky, craft, rug	Bulky, roving
Knit gauge range in St st in 4 in.*	27–32 sts	23–26 sts	21–24 sts	16–20 sts	12–15 sts	6–11 sts
Recommended metric needle size	2.25–3.25 mm	3.25–3.75 mm	3.75–4.5 mm	4.5–5.5 mm	5.5–8 mm	8 mm and larger
Recommended U.S. needle size	1–3	3–5	5–7	7–9	9–11	11 and larger
Crochet gauge range in sc in 4 in.*	21–31 sts	16–20 sts	12–17 sts	11–14 sts	8–11 sts	5–9 sts
Recommended metric hook size	2.25–3.5 mm	3.5–4.5 mm	4.5–5.5 mm	5.5–6.5 mm	6.5–9 mm	9 mm and larger
Recommended U.S. hook size	B/1–E/4	E/4–7	7–I/9	I/9–K/10.5	K/10.5–M/13	M/13 and larger

*The information in this table reflects the most commonly used gauges and needle or hook sizes for the specific yarn categories.

Look for these other *Threads* Selects booklets at www.tauntonstore.com and wherever crafts are sold.

Easy-to-Sew Flowers
EAN: 9781621138259
8 ½ x 10 ⅞, 32 pages
Product# 078017
$9.95 U.S., $9.95 Can.

Easy-to-Sew Gifts
EAN: 9781621138310
8 ½ x 10 ⅞, 32 pages
Product# 078023
$9.95 U.S., $9.95 Can.

Easy-to-Sew Handbags
EAN: 9781621138242
8 ½ x 10 ⅞, 32 pages
Product# 078016
$9.95 U.S., $9.95 Can.

Easy-to-Sew Kitchen
EAN: 9781621138327
8 ½ x 10 ⅞, 32 pages
Product# 078024
$9.95 U.S., $9.95 Can.

Easy-to-Sew Lace
EAN: 9781621138228
8 ½ x 10 ⅞, 32 pages
Product# 078014
$9.95 U.S., $9.95 Can.

Easy-to-Sew Lingerie
EAN: 9781621138235
8 ½ x 10 ⅞, 32 pages
Product# 078015
$9.95 U.S., $9.95 Can.

Easy-to-Sew Pet Projects
EAN: 9781621138273
8 ½ x 10 ⅞, 32 pages
Product# 078018
$9.95 U.S., $9.95 Can.

Easy-to-Sew Pillows
EAN: 9781621138266
8 ½ x 10 ⅞, 32 pages
Product# 078019
$9.95 U.S., $9.95 Can.

Easy-to-Sew Scarves & Belts
EAN: 9781621138211
8 ½ x 10 ⅞, 32 pages
Product# 078013
$9.95 U.S., $9.95 Can.

Easy-to-Sew Skirts
EAN: 9781621138280
8 ½ x 10 ⅞, 32 pages
Product# 078020
$9.95 U.S., $9.95 Can.

Easy-to-Sew Tote Bags
EAN: 9781621138297
8 ½ x 10 ⅞, 32 pages
Product# 078021
$9.95 U.S., $9.95 Can.

Easy-to-Sew Windows
EAN: 9781621138303
8 ½ x 10 ⅞, 32 pages
Product# 078022
$9.95 U.S., $9.95 Can.